Pilgrimages and Prayers Through Poetry

by
Diane Sullivan

To order additional copies of this book, contact:
Xlibris
844-714-8691
www.Xlibris.com
Orders@Xlibris.com

ISBN:	Softcover	978-1-4363-7188-9
	Hardcover	978-1-4363-7189-6
	EBook	978-1-6698-5026-7

Library of Congress Control Number: 2008908492

Print information available on the last page

Rev. date: 09/30/2022

Frank Latino is an Artist, Poet, Author,
Theorist and man of faith.

About the illustrator:

"I was born in 1972 in the city of Florianópolis, an island
located in the south of Brazil. A perfect place for my
creations, the balance between nature and technology. In
a city located in the technology hub of the country, from
very early on I was already involved with computers
and started to work with systems development. With
the emergence of the new media, in 1992 I started my
studies in the famous 3D Studio. That was the beginning
of a passion for digital art, especially for 3D animation.

I participated in numerous television commercials
and I have work shown in galleries across the
web. Memorable characters have earned me
advertising prizes in animation, but nothing is
more important than my passion for work. Visit
my website at www.alexandrelino.com.br"

Printed in the United States
by Baker & Taylor Publisher Services

This book is dedicated to my father
John M. Huebscher.
He taught me how to dream and think in color.

Introduction

This is a book of spiritual poetry. It comes from the heart. It is inspired by the Holy Spirit. This is how it all began:

I was preparing for my first religious pilgrimage. It was in 2004. It was a trip to Italy. The spiritual guide on the trip was Father Dan Kampschneider. Before we embarked on our trip he told all of us that we would all find something unique to each one of us on the pilgrimage. I took this to heart little knowing what an impact it would have on my life. We arrived in Paris, France to catch a plane to Venice, Italy. . As we landed in Paris, Air France played a song on the loud speaker. It was "He Leadeth Me". At the time I thought it sounded as though the angels were serenading us. I took out my journal and started writing. As we landed in Venice I showed it to Father Kampschneider and he suggested I read it after communion as a reflection on the beginning of our pilgrimage. I did. The rest is history.

Since than I have read reflections or poems in St. Peter's Basilica, St. Mary Major, St. John Latern, The church in Ars and several Churches in Ireland. I have written many prayers. The Holy Spirit is definitely inspiring me and working through me. I hope you are inspired a little from these gifts of God. For through my writing they are also gifts for you.

Church of St. Francis Assisi, Italy

St. Peter's Basilica
Rome, Italy

ITALY

A Pilgrim's Prayer
November 3, 2004
Paris, France
To
Venice, Italy

The sound of wheels
slamming and thundering
down upon the pavement;
The soft melodious song
of angels singing us
choruses of "He leadeth me."
Leading us on our spiritual
pilgrimage to know our God.

What will come to light?
to shine in our hearts?
to illuminate our souls?

What whispering will we
hear in the rustling of the wind
through the trees, the tall grasses,
and the rocky mountain sides?

What peace will we feel
from St. Francis of Assisi?
Will his pure love of God
touch our hearts?
Will his wish to honor God
through poverty and humility
cause us to feel the same?

Will the love of St. Anthony
of Padua allow us to find
the virtue each of us needs
to grow in strength, love,
and courage in defending
our God in our society
so immersed in Satan
and his legions of evil?
Anthony, patron of lost things
help us to find the path to God.

Will St. Philip Neri
the laughing saint
bring to us a sense of
mirth and humor?
As he remembered; so
let us remember that
our Creator made the
world to enjoy, to dance,
and to sing of the
glory of God.

Will Peter and Paul
bring to us the desire
to discover the mystery
of God by prayer, by meditation,
by obedience, and by everlasting
trust in God.

Aid us in our journey, Lord.
Grant us the grace to
do all good in your name

to pray, to give, to laugh,

to cry, to suffer, to work,

and to rest
one day
in eternal life with You. AMEN

6

Saint Philip Neri
November 10, 2004
Dedicated to St. Philip Neri Parish

Saint Philip Neri, light of God
light of Rome
light of Florence.

Saint of youth, aid those
of us who work with
the youth of today
so that we appreciate
their energy, their humor,
their honesty, and their curiosity.
Help us guide them
along their path
to God.

Confessor, Father
Help us to look deep
into our souls
so that we may come to
the core of our soul
where God exists in silence
waiting for us to find Him.

Saint of the Virgin Mary,
You conversed with this
sinless handmaiden of the
Lord.
Grant us this love for Mary
who also is waiting to lead
us to her Beloved Son.

Saint Philip Neri, continue to
guide our parish of St. Philip Neri,
today, in Florence in Omaha, Nebraska.
You have given us many holy sisters who taught
in our school, many good lay people who teach
your word to our youth, and very many wonderful
priests in the past and in the present to guide
us on our journey to everlasting life with
God our Creator, Jesus, the Holy Spirit,
and all the holy saints.

Amen

Private Chapel of St. Philip Neri in Church of Santa Maria in Villa Calle

Saints Clare and Francis

Saints of humility
Holy ones of purity
born beneath the skies
of Assisi

Clare, woman of devotion
gentle woman,
humble woman,
wealth and riches had
no meaning for you.
YOU, wanted only God
to Whom you gave praise,
to Whom you prayed for humankind,
to Whom you daily gave thanks.

Saint Clare, pray for us
on this pilgrimage. show us
what you know of God,
of His goodness,
of His forgiveness,
of His all encompassing love
for all His creatures,
for the knowledge of truth,

for the willingness to sacrifice,
to experience pain of both
mind, body, and spirit,
to do for others.

We pray this to you,
Saint Clare, to intercede to God
our Father
    AMEN

Holy Francis, Joy of Assisi
teach us to let loose
of our pride and learn
the practice of humility.

Teach us to love all creatures,
great and small, as you did.
Teach us to appreciate nature's
blue skies,
The rippling waters of the deep seas
the green foliage of the earth,
the purple mountains majesty,
the bright searing sun,
the golden harvest moon,
the twinkling, blinking
light of the stars,
Bright, beautiful blessings
from God.

Francis, your dreams of peace
and good works
are sorely needed in today's world.
It is a world filled with avarice,
impurity and hate.
And yet, there is also a beauty
a beauty of nature,
the innocence of new born babes,
the wisdom of the aged, and
grace through the faith, hope,
charity of many.

Francis, intercede for us, asking
God to shower his gifts upon us
through the intercession of
Saint Clare and You.

    AMEN

Church of St. Francis Assisi, Italy

Saint Catherine of Siena

From Siena you came
with an undeniable
love for Jesus Christ.
You learned to love
by recognizing God
in each of *your*
twenty four
brothers and sisters.
You served your God
with all *your* heart, soul,
mind, and strength.
You suffered the stigmata
with an exquisite joy
for the fact that our Jesus
trusted *you* with his wounds
knowing that from them
y*ou* would exude the
sweetness of suffering with
y*our* God.

Saint Catherine, we pray
that we too might
experience the kind of love
You felt for our Creator God.
Grant us the strength to bear
our sufferings no matter how
small or large, as *you* did.

Grant us purity of mind
constancy of heart,
peace of soul,
and strength of love.

Teach us to know the
Lord, to fight the battle
of evil, to thank our
God and be with
Him always.

AMEN

CATACOMBS

Sighs of the faithful
whispering through the
winding twisting
corridors of the catacombs.

Cries and sighs of babies
laid to rest as if sleeping
while waiting to awaken
in the loving arms
of their God
and to be held again
by long ago mothers and fathers.

Blood spilled for the
glory of God
as Jesus spilled His blood
for the glory of His Father
and our redemption.

Pray for us, all ye holy saints.
We thank you for safekeeping
the Christian faith
centuries upon centuries ago.

We thank you for giving
your lives in unimaginable
ways, so that we too may
imitate the life and suffering
of Jesus Christ.

We thank you for saving the
Holy Eucharist for us as we
must for generations to come.
We came on this pilgrimage—

. . . . each searching for something different,
Perhaps to realize a stronger faith,
to learn more of a special saint,
to see the very beginnings of the growth
of our holy Church,
to see a living saint, John Paul II, who has taught
us so much and is now teaching us how to suffer
for Christ and to grow in our love for God.

Your sacrifices were not in vain.
The Church will always remember you
in the sacrifice of the Mass with the
Communion of Saints . . . . AMEN

Ode to Venice
(In honor of my father, John M. Huebscher)
November 4, 2004

A city so fair
lies on the Adriatic Sea.
A place blessed by God,
a city of saints and popes.
Saint Mark, spreading the
good word of God,
Pope John XXIII
father of Vatican II
growth for the Church.
Pope John Paul I,
a gentle lamb of God
quickly called home by his master
to his heavenly reward.

A city of power and might
century after century
Doges, men of tyranny,
torture, and terror.

A city of architecture
Palaces
Bell towers
and Churches standing
tall and proud, in honor
of God.

A city of art
Veronese, painter of light
Martyrdom of Justine.
Tintoretta, painter of darkness,
The Last Judgment.

A city of exquisite talent
Murano glass ware,
Handmade lace,
Fine soft supple leather
All blessed by God given talents.

A city on the water
peaceful, soothing
Gondolas rowing
forth from the
Adriatic Sea.

Venezia, a gift of beauty
on the landscape of humankind
given
by God to show us that indeed
heaven exists.

Venice, Italy Adriatic Sea

A Pro Life Prayer

The Manger of Bethlehem
A Pro Life Prayer
Saint Mary Major Basilica

Sweet Baby
lying in a manger
Savior of the world.

Manger, cradle,
crib, bassinet, and creche
all words signifying
innocence and purity.

Sweet Babies
innocence personified
God's miracles on earth
alive for all to see.

Mary, holy mother of Jesus,
as you lay your precious Child,
in a manger,
intercede to your beloved Son
that all mothers give birth
to these tiny miracles.

Holy Mary, aid us in our
battle against abortion.
The world needs to see and feel
and hold innocence and love.
in the palm of its hands.

Grant us, O Mary
your love and protection
through your Son, Jesus.

AMEN

Destinations
End of Pilgrimage
November 12, 2004
Airport in Rome

People, tourists, pilgrims,
clergy, children, harried parents
the hustle, the bustle,
the waiting . . . . to reach our destinations.

Waiting for diverse destinations
visiting relatives,
attending a wedding, a class reunion,
a funeral.

What is the final destination?
Where do we hope to go?
Is there a special place to go?
A place where happiness prevails?
A place where peace reigns?
A place where we will never be lonely
or sad again?
A place where love covers us in warmth,
friendliness, and comfort?
A place where God exists?

Questions? Questions? Questions?
Do I believe? Do I not believe?
Questions?

How do we arrive at this place
of wonder and promise?
Is it simply through believing in God?
Is it through doing for others?
Is it through the Holy Eucharist
and other sacraments divine?
Is it as Saint Francis says,
"Faith and Good Deeds"?

How do we come to God?
We love Him with our whole hearts, our whole bodies,
our whole minds, and our whole strengths.
we love our neighbors as we love ourselves.
Thus we come to the wonder and awesomeness of our God.

AMEN

Monastaboice. Example of the High Crosses of Ireland.

Cliffs of Moher

Ode to Irish Monasticism

Pillars of God
strong stalwart
men, modern apostles
of the Son.

Monasterboice
    Fifth century
    house of God
    founded by St. Buitre.
Towers
    signifying the Glory of God;
High Crosses
    describing the life of Christ
    and God's covenants with
    his people.
Muirdach's Cross
Dysert Cross and
High Cross of Ahenny.

Hill of Slane,
    birthplace of the paschal fire
    lit by Patrick challenging ancient
    chieftains and pagan customs at Tara.

Clonmacnoise,
    monastery on the River Shannon
    founded by St. Ciarron,
    scholarship and piety
    keeping alive the history of
    the Church during the dark ages.

St. Columban,
    Father of missionaries
    carrying throughout the world
    in the footsteps of the apostles
    the Word of God.

Without these pillars of strength
Where would Christianity be?
    Sacred manuscripts,
    Book of Kells,
    Tall Crosses,
    Missionaries,
    All keepsakes and reminders
    of our Church's history,
    the story of Jesus, our Savior.

Slane Hill Ruins of Monastery Dating Back to St. Patrick

Circle of Love

In the land of emerald green,
in the land of the ancient
leprechauns and druids,
in the land of holy saints
Padraig, Brendan, and Brigid,
There lies a sacred circle which
I have seen, felt, and experienced.

It lies near the village of Ballymoe.
Beneath the awnings of ancient
gnarled white tarn trees.
At first glance this holy space
seemed rather ordinary, nothing
        special.
But as I sat on logs and some on stones
        a silence came upon all.
A silence that tells one, "Be in *awe* for
        holy people were here"
The Holy Spirit came upon me and showed
me a piece of history in times of persecution.
For there, in this space, priests had come to
celebrate Mass, sheltered by the shrubbery
and white tarn trees, celebrating Mass for the
holy people of God, defying all civil authority.

It was a cold damp windy day when I sat there
        attending Mass.
The Rhua was upon me. It came in a gale of wind
        entering my soul with a certainty
        that God, himself, was present with me.

Circles of love exist around the world in many
        ways and places.
Do we see our own circle at Mass on Sundays?
Do we see our circle at family dinners?
Do we see a circle in a park full of children?
Do we see a circle in a home for the elderly?
        We, too, have our holy circles.

Let us pray that we recognize them in our
daily lives and turn them into holy places.

The Rhua of Ireland

And the Lord said,
"I will send you the Spirit to be
with you until I return again."
        And a great wind
came upon them, the sacred wind
        of the Spirit.

        Can you feel this
breath upon you in the land
of Padraig, Brendan, and Brigid?
        Can you?
Didn't you hear and feel
it on the Cliffs of Moher?
Mightn't it be the strong
Atlantic gales sent from
God to remind us of the
majesty of His creation
and our duty to care for it?

        Can you feel the Spirit in the
mellow breeze of Ballentubber,
the eight centuries old church
which has continually celebrated
the saving Paschal Mystery
of Jesus our Redeemer?
Mightn't it be the Spirit carried
in the soft breeze sent by God to
remind us that He will always
be faithful in His love for us
as we must be to Him?

        Can you feel the rhua in
the lilting wind at Inch Abbey on
the shores of the River Quoile?
        Look carefully! Can you?
Can you gleam the shadow of
of the Cistercians going about their daily
work? See! To the Left. A monk
is taking bread from the oven.
        Can you hear the chanting
of the Liturgy of Hours being
carried on the breeze? Mightn't it be
that we need to center our lives on
our God in our busy modern schedules?

Can you feel this Rhua being sent
from the Father to ensure us of the
goodness of our God in his heavenly
message to His people who long ago
knew to make use of the resources by
digging the peat, drying it, and using it
to burn as fuel on the bitter cold winter
    night?

    Can you feel the Spirit whirling
around ancient Round Towers? The holy
monks who painstakinly drew and illumined
letter after letter, page after page,
manuscript after manuscript so that the world
would come to know and to receive the Word
    of His Son Incarnate.

Mightn't it too be a sign that we too
must keep this sacred
inheritance of Christianity for
our children's children.
For often doesn't it seem as though
Christianity may be going through
another dark age?
As the monks in the old
Gaelic Round Towers strove
to preserve the Word of God
so must we by our example,
tradition and prayer.

And so the Rhua blows and breathes
over the heavenly Emerald Isle
        as
He blows and breathes over the entire
        world.

O Holy Spirit, come upon us and hear
        our prayers.
Renew in us the fire of your love.
Grant us the grace to grow in your
abundant gifts and fruits so that we
may use what is given us to the greater
honor and glory of God.
        Amen

FRANCE

Garden at Home of St Therese,
Little Flower

Eiffel Tower, Paris, France

24

Pilgrimage to France
September 14, 2005

O Hare Airport, Chicago, 14 of September, 2005

As we embark on this wondrous pilgrimage
through the country often referred to as the eldest
daughter of the Church, we will come to realize we
are not on a journey to find Christ for He is already
dwelling within us.
In the words of St. Augustine, "Late I loved You,
O Beauty, so ancient and so new, late have I loved You!
You were within me and I was outside and there I sought
for You. You were with me, and I was not with You".
In our pilgrimage let us realize that God is always with us.
As we travel through France we will see how God was with the Cure
of Ars; a humble sweet man who struggled to become a priest,
who prayed to convert his parish, who loved God above all, and
whose devotion to Mary caused him to say, "No grace can come from
heaven without first passing through her hands".

We will see Therese of Lisieux, the Little Flower.
As a child she knew that she belonged to God. A simple
life she lived fulfilling her destiny by doing God's will in
small seemingly unimportant acts. God was with her. She
died young and sent roses showered down from heaven to show
her love and determination to continue God's work in heaven.

We will see St. Vincent de Paul, a learned man, who often
earned his way through the seminary tutoring children of the wealthy.
He became a man who longed to help the poor, the homeless, the liminal.
He began the Daughters of Charity with St. Louise de Merilac.

All saints of France, who were not looking for God, but with God
found the way to eternal life simply by opening their hearts to His word.
Let us pray that we find the way in which God is with each one of us.
We see that He accompanied St. John Vianney, St. Vincent de Paul, Catherine of
Laboure, valiant St. Joan of Arc, St. Bernadette, and St. Margaret Mary.
We pray that we too receive the grace to open our hearts to God and follow
the footsteps of these saints into eternal life. We ask this of Jesus Christ.
Amen

I AM GOD

Normandy, France 15 of September 2005

Who is God? you ask

I am God, the creator of all.
the round yellow disc of flaming
gases high in the bright blue sky
to keep you warm by day.
The creator of the black night sky
full of twinkling stars and the crescent
moon to keep your fears of darkness at bay.

I am the creator of tall majestic trees to give
you shade from the sometimes searing heat,
of trees that bear fruit so that you may taste
of the sweetness of my love.

The creator of waters of the deep oceans and seas
to give life to your world by the fish in the sea.
I give rain and snow to flow into the rivers and lakes
to quench your thirst as I needed to quench my thirst
on the cross at Golgatha.
This water which nourishes your body also nourished
your soul through the waters of Baptism where you are
cleansed and become my children.

I am the creator of animals, large and small. Some you
use as beasts of burden, some you use to nourish your bodies;
some you use for companionship, a beloved pet.

I am the creator of all who fought for freedom on the shores
of Normandy and Omaha Beach. I was with them that cold
day. I blessed them. They did not die in vain. Be proud.
but do not forget that I also created all of mankind, all soldiers
who fought that day for are they not also made in my image
and likeness? Remember that I am forgiving and loving God.
I too was with them as I am now around the world where
mankind continues to fight.

I Am Your God.

American Cemetary in Normandy, France

Your Humble Servant
Cure of Ars

My God, my heart is heavy with love for you.
       I am a humble man, a simple man.
I struggled and struggled to learn Latin so I
could become your priest. Finally, I made it with your help.
       I am a humble man, a simple man.
I am now your servant, your priest. I am in your hands.
My new parish of Ars, O Lord, help me, pray for me.
My wish is to convert them to your greater glory.
What can I do for them? What can I tell them?
What? O Lord, What did you say? Ah, yes . . .
I can tell them to always pray as God commands.
Give yourself to God, put yourself in His presence,
but "do not worry, do not worry," for our Jesus
will care for you.

The people are needy my lord, there is so much to do,
so many to pray for, so many to confess.
I am tired Lord. I want to leave and devote myself
in prayer and adoration before the Blessed Sacrament.
I will leave tonight.
Oh, the people, my Lord, the people.
They bring me back to Ars three times now. Are you
telling me to stay put, my Lord?
       I am a humble man, a simple man.
       I will stay at Ars, as you wish.

What more can I give? I eat little. I sleep little.
I need the time to pray. I need the time to be in the
confessional, to meet my people's needs, to read their
souls, to advise them.

I tell them "Do not offer anything
you cannot offer to God."

Thirty some years in Ars,
seventeen hours a day in
the confessional, thousands and
thousands of God's people
turning back towards God through
repentance of their sins.

I, your humble servant, am tired.
My God, take me home to You.
Ah hhh hhh hhh, my Lord, Merci."

O sweet humble St. John Vianney
intercede to God that all priests
love as You loved God. Grant to
all our parish priests the grace to
continue in their humble service,
in your gentle way. Grant them serenity,
peace, and the love of all God's people.
Amen

St. John Vianney in Ars, France
Patron of Parish Priests

NEW DESTINATIONS

As we leave Lourdes before the dawning of the
day with hearts enlarged with a holy love,
We leave with a feeling of awe and reverence.
We know we have seen and felt a sacred place
in the very core of our souls.
We know we have been where God has been.
For where His mother is so too is the Son.

What are we taking with us from this
sacred pilgrimage on which we have journeyed?
New friends? Yes indeed!
Fond memories? Of course!
A sense of being closer to God?
How perfect that would be!
A wish to be more like the saints?
Why Not?
We are all called to be saints
through our Baptism, Confirmation,
and Holy Eucharist.
But how? How can we possibly be like the
ones we have seen?
Listen to the words of some of the saints we have seen.
St. Therese says, "To love is to give all to Him
and to give yourself to all"".
Why can't we do this?
St. Joan of Arc says, "I ask first of all, to make peace.
If one is not prepared to make that peace, I am quite ready
to fight for it".
Why can't we first try to make peace?
St. Margaret Mary was given the privilege to know
the Sacred Heart of Jesus.
Why can't we make the nine first Fridays?
St. Vincent de Paul reminds us that we are
indeed our brother's keeper.
Do we feed the hungry? Do we shelter the homeless?
Why can't we?
St. John Vianney says, "If one thinks well, one cannot live
and offend a God who is so good, who has taken such a
good heart and who loves us so much".
Why can't we love God as the cure of Ars did?
St. Bernadette simply says, :Love God, children.
That is what is important."
More love. Can we do it?

As we touch ground in our home states
let us pray to God that we adopt a saint
for one year and discover how our blessings
from God grow into a spiritual bouquet that
is worthy to offer to God and Mary his mother.

St. Bernadette, Convent in Nevers, France

PRAYERS

And God Smiled

Did you know
that a miraculous event
occurred on February 10th,
2008, right here in the Big O,
 The River City?

It involved a relatively small
number of people when one
looks at the whole of society.

There was a parade, a most holy
parade, a parade of the people of
God, coming to meet God's
Shepherd, Archbishop Eldon Curtiss.

They came of all ages filled with an
 inner joy.
The elderly, bundled up against the
 blistering winter cold;
The middle-aged, costumed in all
 manner of dress;
The teens, dressed in jeans and sweaters
 the uniform of their age.
The little children, God's special people,
dressed in white communion clothes, lilac
 dresses, suits, and jeans.
 They all came and God smiled.

They came of all races, cultures, and
 social and economical classes.
They came filled with an inner knowledge
 that God views them all the same.
Some were nervous; some were prayerful.
Others were expectant; others came in wonder.
Many came in hope; many came in thanksgiving.
The infirmed came slowly, the younger more quickly,
and the children came skipping, nearly dancing.
 They all came and God smiled.

They came out of a deep longing for the
Truth, the Word, and the Light.
They have read, they have listened,
they have heard, they have seen,
and they have felt the Essence of God.

He has touched their hearts and swirled
down into the inner most being of their
soul and took root.

They came to be welcomed into the Holy
Catholic Church by the shepherd of Jesus,
our Archbishop.
They came and God smiled.

The Light

"Warm, caressing,
enveloping light.
Light of love,
peace, safety.

Watery, rocking,
dark cocoon safe,
but not sure,
Where is the Light?

Intense pushing,
noise, sliding,
bright, glaring,
cold, harsh lights.
Where am I?

Warmth, arms
around me, soft,
cooing sounds of love.
Eyes of a woman
looking at me
with a glimpse of that
other soft warm light
showing through her eyes.
Is this a mother's love?

Old, tired, aching bones
searching my mind for
a long ago feeling
of a forgotten light
different from earthly light.
Where is this Light?

A dark, swirling
funnel shaped
tunnel, so dark.
Speed, faster and faster.
Wait! A light!
a warm, caressing,
enveloping light
of pure love.

Home with God
I am home with God"

Blessed Sacrament of Jesus

My God, My Jesus,
I kneel before You
in the Blessed Sacrament.
I praise You.
I adore You.
I thank You.
I love You

I notice the placement of Your
precious Body in the monstrance
with its golden rays shining forth
from the center of the all Being,
YOU

Placed on Mary's altar
under her heart as You
were in her womb, safe,
warm and loved.
She looks upon You
with the pure love of
a holy mother.

From the corner of my right eye.
I see You hanging on the cross
suffering unbearable pain.
Every bone hurts, every muscle hurts,
every fiber in Your Body
hurts with an exquisite
pulsating pain.
You look down upon Your mother,
Mary.

Did You think?
"Help Me, my mother,
Make my hurts go away.
I can't stand this pain.
Hold Me, Comfort Me, Tell Me
all will be all right.
Please, my mother, help me.
That's what mothers do.
Help Me, help Me, Please!"

You look upwards and cry out,
"My Father, My Father,
Why have You abandoned Me?"
Then You look outward and see
humankind for all time.
You see Adam, Moses, Peter,
John, and the others. You see children
playing throughout the ages, farmers plowing
the fields, and mail carriers delivering the mail.
You see wars, famine, plague, bombs,
and terrorists of every kind.
You see Saints, clergy, lay people,
all working for You.
You see all and think,
"Ah, yes, I remember now, my Father,
Thy will be done. I am sent to die for them
that they might be saved. The love of my Father is great,
and my Father's love is my love, and the Spirit's love is our
love and so I die..
Into your hands I commend my Spirit."

Mary looks upon the cross and thinks,
"Oh, my Son, my Life, my God.
Do not think I do not wish
I could stop your pain,
could kiss it away,
could hold You close
to my heart
soothing You.
I can not. It is not in the Divine Plan.
I must follow "thy will be done to me
according to thy word."
You know it. You follow it.
I will not stop loving You.
We will be together again."

I look again and see Jesus's
Body reposing under the heart of Mary.

Is this an accident,
this placement
of the Blessed Sacrament?
I think not-for today—it told me
a story of Love
between Father, Mother, and Son.

The preceding poem was written during an hour of Adoration
in my parish church, St. Philip Neri.

Water

H_2O, a small atom,
so minute, yet the
source of all life.

$H_2O + 32F$
dropping on mountain
peaks, leaving a white
icing on the crown of
the earth.

H_2O + a warm atmosphere,
rain refreshing the parched
earth allowing seeds to grow,
plants to mature, trees to leaf
out in hues of green, the green
of life, hope, and growth
allowing God's animals
His gift of life.

$H_2O+NaCl+$, the mighty seas
and oceans of the world from
which all life began; amoebas,
crustaceans, amphibians, mammals,
all in the chain of life.

H_2O+ morning dew glistening
on the fresh green grass
inviting us to a lazy fun filled
day enjoying the nature of God.

H_2O+ coffee beans
a much needed
wake up call.

H_2O+ tea leafs,
a relaxing soothing drink
to calm oneself and our
bodies after a hard day's work.

H_2O+ plant cells,
oranges, grapes, lemons,
sweetness and joy.

H_2O+ God's blessing,
holy water to remind us of God
and his gift of life.

$H_2O+Baptism$, source of
spiritual life, new life,,
sacred life bringing us
back to the Father.

$H_2O+grapes+Jesus$
fruit of the vine,
blood of Christ.

H_2O
quenching, cleansing, cascading
within our souls, nourishing
our spiritual life so that one day
we may enter the kingdom
of God.

The Wonders of God

Oh, to see the wonders of God
in the eyes of a child!
The glory of God in a flickering
lightning bug,
the movement of God on a
hopping toad,
the golden burst of sunlight
in the radiance of a dandelion.
The discovery of the Creator God
in a small boy's
eyes as he watches an ant crawl
across the ground.
The unconditional love of God
as a puppy licks a child's
face with abandoned love.
The warmth of God, as a hot
sweaty child, with a grin on his face,
opens his tightly clenched fist, hands you
a ladybug and says, "I love you."
The refreshing God, as children gleefully
run under the hose to cool off on a
hot sweltering summer day,
The dreaming God as small children
lay in the grass and watch dinosaurs, castles,
and unicorns float across the sky.
You and and I see clouds
but God shows them much more.
The joyful God as the ice-cream man
ding dongs up and down the street

selling sweet delights for
gleeful children-
Oh! to again be like a child,
to see love in our neighbors,
to see the good in a much needed rain,
to hear the noise of children in the park,
as a beautiful symphony of joy,
to see the beauty of a dandelion, thistle,
and goldenrod..not as weeds, but as
flowers which they truly are,
to see the clouds as pictures
painted by God, not as harbingers
of dangerous storms,
to see turtles as always ready to
be called into their homes;
not as freaky left overs
from the age of dinosaurs.

I once read the the stars are the
eyes of heaven and that
the flowers are the eyes of earth.
What a beautiful thought!

Oh, God, as children
can see what we often
do not see, grant us the grace to renew
in ourselves the wonders of your world
and as St. John of The Cross said, "the
traces of who You are".

Servants of God

"Born to be free"
calls forth the media
through the air waves
of time,
"Not so," responds the the
eternal air waves
from time primeval
to the age of Aquarius.

"Servants of Yaweh,
the Almighty One,"
echoes relentlessly
from the twinkling
stars so carefully placed
in the broad spectrum
of our universe.

Celestial bodies, servants of God?
"Proudly so," pulsates
each blinking light in the
vastness of space.

"Servants of the Great
Creator, the Awesome One,"
is expelled with each breath
from the tiniest seahorses
to the majestic Barbara with
his last breath of service.

Animals, servants of God?
"Proudly so" announces each
breath inhaled and exhaled.

Servants of the Absolute Artist,
the Beautiful One, silently felt
in the soft caressing breeze
of the meadows filled with
wild flowers nodding their heads
to the cherished touch of their
artist, God the Creator.

Plants, servants of God?
"Proudly so," waves multicolored
hues of crops in fields and forests,
in jungles and mountains
throughout the earth, feeding the
people of God.

Humankind, servants of God?
"Proudly so," for our service
can be seen in the hands of
artists, musicians, builders
and in the healing touches
of the emaciated, scabbed,
beaten bodies of the downtrodden
in all societies.
Service is seen in mouths via
singing soft lullabies,
praying the rosary,
teaching tolerance,
laughing and crying
with all people in
God's world
Service is seen in human ears:
listening to God's voice in the
cry of a newborn babe,
hearing the stories of the
wise aged,
the fantasies of the young,
the cry of the poor,
the pain of the sick,
the despair of the imprisoned.

Humankind, servants of God.
Yes indeed, in every thought,
word, and action enacted by
all God's creatures,
big and small,
created to serve their God.

O Holy One

O holy One,

O pure gentle Jesus,

O comforter Spirit,

Be my comfort in
difficult times.

Be my companion
in quiet loneliness.

Be my mentor
in my confused
puzzling moments.

Be my joy
when no one else sees
the beauty which surrounds them.

Be my hope
in a world bent with
fear and despair.

Be my truth
in a world which does
not believe in what it
cannot see

Be my love
in a world filled with
distrust and hate.

Be my life source
in all that I do
in my thought, words,
deeds and actions.

Amen

A Smile's Power

The most beautiful image
of the human face is
a smile.

The face softens;
the eyes come alive.
Age lessens and a
youthfulness appears.

The wonder of God
images itself onto the face.

Smile at a lonely person;
watch his hardened face
slowly relax into a smile.
You have made his day.
You have given him back his dignity
and filled him with a sense
of worthiness and love.

Smile and say "thank you"
to an employee in a
restaurant, a clerk in a store,
or a laborer on the street.
He looks at you with a frown
on his face. A smile forms and
he says, "Well, you have a good
day now".
You have given him a reason to
continue his work. Perhaps, you
have given him the only smile he will
receive that day

Smile at a mother with three
small children; one is holding
her hand, one is holding on
to her leg, and a baby is in her
arms.

Smile at her and tell her how
precious her children are.
She may sigh with frustration for a
moment but a smile of pleasure
overcomes her face as she
thanks you.
You have given her an affirmation
of doing God's will and the
honor of raising the children
of God.

Smile at an ill-tempered
negative co-worker.
You know that she has problems.
She is bitter, her husband left her,
and she seems incapable of
seeing good in anyone.
Yet, you know she is a good
worker and completes her work.
Smile, she may not smile back
in the forseeable future.
However, this cantankerous
co-worker will carry the
image of your smile in her
heart and one day it will
break through into a beautiful smile.

Never underestimate the power
of a smile. A smile is equal to
the warmth of the sun melting a
mountain glacier.
A smile is the fragrance of a
rose garden wafting through
the your whole being into your
soul.

A smile is a choice God gives you.
You can choose to use those special
facial muscles and create a frown
or a smile.

What will you choose?

45

John Paul II, the Great

Who was this man who spoke with
compassion, piety, and truth
in the many tongues of the world?
He spoke the Word of God.

Who was this man who saw with
clarity, foresight, and love
all people of God?
He saw with the Eyes of God.

Who was this man who heard the
cry of God's people? He heard
with knowledge, consideration, and mercy.
He heard with the Ears of God.

Who was this man who was able to detect
the odor of evil in the world—the culture
of death, moral decay, and ridicule for those
who work against injustice?
He smelled with the Nose of God.

Who was this man who reached out to
touch the downtrodden, the poor, and
the suffering?
He touched with the Hands and Heart of God.

This man was a gift given to us by God
through the Holy Spirit. He was a man
beloved by many and feared by many.
He was a man with the courage to follow
the faith as Jesus desired.
He was a man who truly imitated his Lord,
Jesus Christ
with his whole heart, his whole strength,
his whole mind, and his whole soul.

He was born into a era of genocide,
fratricide, and unmitigated evil.
He was a man born into the divine plan
of God, a plan to fight this mounting
horror with love, mercy, and forgiveness
as his Jesus taught.

He was a man who taught the world
to love the innocent, the elderly,
the unborn, and the handicapped
without reservation as to their
usefulness to the world.

He was a man who laughed
played, sang, danced.
He taught the truth, loved all,
and prayed daily.

He was a man who taught us to live
in God, to enjoy and care for God's creations,
to suffer as Jesus, and to die in the presence
of God.

Nuestro Papá Juan Pablo II,
Vaya con Dios.

John Paul the Great, Nov. 2004

Anne and Joachim
Dedicated to All Grandparents

Anne and Joachim, you were blessed
to be the holy parents of a singularly
holy woman.

Your child would become the mother
of the long awaited Messiah
and your grandson.

As you watched Mary grow
did you know?
Did you know that God
had bestowed upon you
the mother of a truly blessed grandchild?
Did you know that through prayers,
examples, and teachings, your child, Mary,
would become the most praised mother
to ever live?

Did you know that she was conceived
without sin and therefore became
the only human ever to be worthy
to carry the Son of God?

Did you know and hold your
precious grandson?
As you rocked him, did he
look up into your eyes with all trust
and love causing your hearts to melt?

Did you think, "My grandson is
the absolute most precious of
all babies." "He will become
famous in the world".
Indeed he did.

Did you smile at him, play with him,
tickle him, and make him laugh?
Did you kiss his hurts, make his
sweet cakes, and let him stay up
later than would mom and dad?

Did you know that your sweet daughter
and grandson would suffer beyond all
imaginable pain in spirit and body?

Anne and Joachim, patrons of
grandparents, grant that my
grandchildren and all grandchildren
throughout the world grow to know,
love, and serve your grandson
and be with him for all eternity.
Amen

48

BEHOLD!

Behold! A baby
lies in a manger,
swaddled in cloth,
surrounded by straw,
and warmed by the
moist warm breaths
of nearby animals . . . .
His creatures.

But, Wait! Wasn't He the Son
        of God?

Behold, A baby
who cried from
hunger and had
to nurse at His
mother's breast . . .
as do all His creatures.

But, Wait! Wasn't He the Son
        of God?

Behold, A baby
whose body functioned
as all babies do.
He must be changed, cleansed,
and kept dry . . . .
as do all His creatures.

But, Wait! Wasn't He the Son
        of God?

Behold, A baby
who felt the cold
experienced pain
and grief, who
cooed and smiled . . .
as do all His creatures.

But, Wait! Wasn't He the Son
        of God?

Behold! A baby
who must flee
with His mother
and father to a far
away land in order
to escape death . . .
as often do His
creatures.

But, Wait! Wasn't He the Son
        of God?

The Incarnation,
GOD MADE FLESH,
gift of all gifts,
from the DIVINE
to the human,
the total love of the
baby's ABBA.
All, so that we might live.

My God, How Great Thou Art!

Printed in the United States
by Baker & Taylor Publisher Services